Virgin MoDERN iCoNS

MARC BOLAN

Acknowledgements

With very grateful thanks to Philip Dodd, Morse Modaberi,
Helen Johnson and to Keith Richmond, Michael Heatley,
Northdown Publishing and the staff of the National Sound
Archive for their help in the research of this book.

Paul Du Noyer started his career on *NME*, before joining the launch team of
Q magazine. He was editor of *Q* between 1990 and 1992, and then became the
founding editor of the hugely influential monthly magazine *Mojo*, picking up an Editor
of the Year award in 1994. He left *Mojo* in 1995, but remains a contributing editor.

First published in 1997 by
Virgin Publishing Ltd
332 Ladbroke Grove
London W10 5AH.

Modern Icons series conceived and developed
for and with Virgin Publishing Ltd by Flame Tree Publishing,
a part of The Foundry Creative Media Company Limited,
The Long House, Antrobus Road, Chiswick, London W4 5HY.

Modern Icons series © Virgin Publishing Ltd 1997
Text © Flame Tree Publishing.

ISBN 1 85227 683 5

A catalogue record for this book is available from the British Library.

Virgin MoDERN iCoNS

MARC BOLAN

Introduction by Paul Du Noyer

CONTENTS

CONTENTS

INTRODUCTION

Whatever happened to the teenage dream? Barely half a year had passed since the formal abdication of the Beatles in Spring 1970. But there had been a dull, aching void in the heart of British pop music for much longer than that. In fact, not since the glory days of Beatlemania – an era consigned to history by the group's retirement from touring in 1966 – had there been a genuine spell of pure pop hysteria to enliven the scene and brighten our days. For sheer flash and glamour, some would say that nothing had equalled the first fantastical starburst of Elvis Presley and rock'n'roll itself, more than a decade previously.

Had T. Rex not come along at that precise moment, perhaps, it would have been necessary to invent them. But Marc Bolan, who really *was* T. Rex, was not a man to miss his moment. After all, he had been waiting for it since his early childhood. And when that magical window of opportunity presented itself, Marc Bolan effectively invented himself. In the space of a few short months in 1970, the pint-sized East End mod, until then a lisping, blissed-out flower child of the hippie revolution, took decisive steps that would transform him into the first full-blown rock phenomenon of the new decade. As suddenly as the flick of a switch, he ran a powerful surge of electrical voltage through his hitherto gentle, cross-legged music, dramatically revamped his act, promptly abbreviated its name and, standing to his full height, boldly announced the arrival of Marc Bolan, Superstar. Beginning with his first hit record, 'Ride A White Swan', T. Rex came to rule the pop charts. And everywhere you looked, the madness was back.

It may look inevitable in hindsight, but before the outpouring of fan frenzy that was quickly dubbed 'T. Rextasy', nobody knew if pop would ever see such scenes again. The once juvenile art form had aged by then. In its maturity, it had deepened and diversified. The Beatles had grown beards and grown mystical; Bob Dylan brought poetical complexity; Jimi Hendrix introduced astonishing virtuosity; the Rolling Stones seemed to represent something savage and extreme. Between these new rock deities and the Sixties generation who worshipped them, there arose a movement so all-pervading that it was called the counter-culture. Even black American music was moving away from the eternal verities of gospel, dance and good times. In response, a baffled and

anxious entertainment industry tried to fill the vacuum left by this collective loss of innocence. There were cleverly manufactured 'teenybop' treats, such as the Monkees, and conveyor-belt hits, like the Archies's 'Sugar Sugar'. Older people, alienated by the chaos, were served a safe diet of dinner-jacketed crooners, to soothe the onset of middle age. But nothing stuck. Compared with the might of the Woodstock Nation, pop music was enfeebled. It seemed in terminal decline.

It was Marc Bolan's achievement − and really Bolan's alone − to turn this picture on its head. In Britain at least, he ushered in a new dawn for popular music. Perhaps the abiding sadness of his later life was that his message found no ready response in America, the rock'n'roll Valhalla of his considerable ambitions. But his influence went deep, just the same. If nothing else, he lived to see the birth of punk rock, which might never have happened without him. And punk rock did change everything that came after it, all over the world. By the Nineties there were musicians across America who embraced the T. Rex legend and recognised the unsung part he played in shaping their own heritage, from the stadium theatrics of Kiss to the sharpened pop instincts of Eighties new wave.

Back in his own hey-day, the early Seventies, Bolan didn't lack detractors. Most rock journalists were grateful for the boost of newsworthiness he'd given to a sleepy scene. But there were plenty of others – some of them admirers of his old group Tyrannosaurus Rex – who condemned his 'betrayal' of underground values, sneered at his musical simplicity and mistrusted the stagey posturing of his new persona. In retrospect, their unease reflected a certain disappointment with the progress of rock music. Before Bolan, pop's history was seen as linear – onwards and upwards – but he showed that it was cyclical. Consciously or not, Marc identified a disenfranchised generation, too young to believe in the advances of the Sixties, indifferent to its ideals and, above all, desperate for something they could call their own. The young kids did not want to learn from pop history. They wanted to re-live it all over again.

Actually the smarter rock musicians of 1970 had their own inkling of rock's limitations. After the dazzling innovations of psychedelia, taken to their zenith by the Beatles's 'Sgt. Pepper' album in 1967, there had been a steady drift back to basics. Whether guided by nostalgia for their own teenage years in the Fifties, or by the fashion for 'rootsy' forms like country, blues and Southern funk, figures like Bob Dylan and Eric Clapton embraced the 'authenticity' of acts such as The Band and Credence Clearwater Revival. With almost their parting words to the world, the Beatles sang 'Get Back', over a chugging, primitive beat. This was a trend that Bolan tapped into. He also sensed that what the greying patriarchs could not supply now was youthful energy and glamour. It's enormously symbolic that the first figureheads to publicly endorse T. Rex were the ex-Beatles themselves. John Lennon was enchanted by Bolan's grasp of Fifties rock dynamics, the shrewdly populist Paul McCartney was equally complimentary and Ringo Starr became Marc's first celebrity camp-follower, documenting T. Rextasy from the front row with his cine-camera.

Bolan's great good fortune was to be exactly the right age to understand the point rock had reached, and to exploit it. He was pretty enough to look the part, sufficiently talented to make the formula work, and had the drive to knock down the obstacles in his path.

Born to working-class Londoners in 1947, the young Mark Feld (as he was then) played out his rock'n'roll fantasies in a neighbourhood band called Susie & The Hula Hoops. He must have been profoundly interested to watch one of their number, a local girl named Helen Shapiro, go on to become one of Britain's first teenage stars. (She later toured with the Beatles, whose arrival rather coincided with her decline.) His childhood idols were the first wave of US rock'n'rollers, including Elvis, Eddie Cochran and Chuck Berry, and their imprint would never fade from his mind. After that, as a teenager obsessed with clothes, he was a natural recruit to the mod cause – a cliquey élite of fashion-conscious youth gangs – and his comely appearance won him a brief career in modelling. By the early Sixties, however, he was drawn towards the beatnik troubadour style of Bob Dylan, cutting a folkish single under the name Toby Tyler.

In 1965, he was one more young hustler on the lower rungs of the London pop business. Decca Records let him make a few singles – including 'The Wizard', which he liked to pretend was inspired by a mysterious magician in Paris – but to no effect. An observant entrepreneur, Simon Napier-Bell, took a shine to the boy who had now re-styled himself Marc Bolan. The manager placed him in a struggling psychedelic combo, John's Children. This liaison was short-lived, but Bolan did write their strangely beguiling single 'Desdemona', adding a back-up vocal in the unique, quivering bleat that became his trademark.

Though his career appeared to stall, Bolan never stopped learning. Suddenly without a band, or even equipment, he formed an acoustic duo with one Steve Peregrine Took. Now his fancy was for the most extravagant trappings of hippie culture. The pair affected other-worldly feyness. Bolan strummed and warbled, while Took's bongos pattered like mice behind the skirting boards. Always an insatiable reader, Marc recycled elements from the fantasy authors J. R. R. Tolkien and C. S. Lewis, as well as all the poetry and ancient mythology he could absorb, fashioning a magical landscape populated by dwarves, unicorns, warriors and fair maidens. He grew his coal-black curls into the corkscrew mane of a Botticelli swain. The duo teamed up with a young American producer, Tony Visconti, to make albums with florid titles such as 'My People Were Fair And Had Sky In Their Hair . . . But Now They're Content To Wear Stars On Their Brows' and 'Prophets Seers And Sages The Angels Of Ages'. Only the group's name told of the fierce ambition that burned in Bolan's breast. He called it Tyrannosaurus Rex – after the biggest, baddest creature he could think of. Yet there were hints in the music itself of Bolan's attachment to classic pop: hot-rod car images and 12-bar chord sequences were a feature and the third album, 'Unicorn', has subtle echoes of Phil Spector. By the fourth album, 'A Beard Of Stars', Bolan had replaced the wayward Took with a more compliant sidekick, percussionist

Mickey Finn, whose handsome gypsy looks were every bit as marketable as Marc's. He also introduced some electric guitar to the mix, albeit cautiously, and the final Tyrannosaurus Rex single, 'By The Light Of A Magical Moon', fades to the overdubbed sound of screaming teenage girls. Bolan's hour was finally at hand.

When Mickey and Marc were next heard on the airwaves, their name had lost four syllables while their sound had picked up several decibels. Plain 'T. Rex' was the credit on their October 1970 single 'Ride A White Swan', an irresistible slice of electric bop that sailed to Number 2. It was scarcely a hard rock number, but beneath the velvet glove you caught the first glint of an iron fist. Three months later Marc was celebrating his first Number 1, 'Hot Love' and forming a four-piece band to take him to the next level. Now beefed up by a real rhythm section – drummer Bill Legend and bassist Steve Currie – T. Rex was

ready to play perfect pop with all the muscle of a proper, grown-up band. They consolidated with an unbeatable run of powerful, full-tilt teen-rock anthems: 'Get It On', 'Jeepster', 'Telegram Sam' and 'Metal Guru'. The same period saw Bolan's two strongest albums, 'Electric Warrior' and 'The Slider'.

While it lasted, throughout 1971 and for most of 1972, Bolan's domination of British pop was absolute. His portrait adorned the pin-up magazines. T. Rex toured the country and brought pandemonium to every town, as girls screamed and fainted in the classic manner. To these young females, Marc was part romantic prince, a beautiful fantasy, and part strutting sex god – a novel composite of wan, feminised minstrel and rampant, macho boogie man. He loved to replay the guitar heroics of the recently-deceased Jimi Hendrix, to bump and grind like any grizzled rocker. But he scorned the drab, beards-and-denim aesthetic of the new rock establishment. Marc wore satin and silk, with perhaps a feather boa and some silver glitter on his cheeks. He was not a hiccuping pixie any more, but a motor-mouthing street poet. He liked to flaunt his gorgeousness, and nobody had ever seen his like before.

Old acquaintances felt repelled by Bolan's new, armour-plated exterior. His cockiness had once been charming, but could now seem obnoxious. Cynics would note how narrow his musical palette had become, as he re-worked his favourite riffs one more time. The UK charts were suddenly full of acts that bore his imprint: Slade, Sweet, Gary Glitter and the rest. But Bolan's commercial instincts started to falter, 'Children Of The Revolution', 'Solid Gold Easy Action', 'Twentieth Century Boy' and 'The Groover' were all hits, but the magic was fading.

By the time he sang 'Whatever happened to the Teenage Dream?', the line sounded like an elegy to himself. By 1973, even his hard-core teenybop following was breaking up, either outgrowing him or moving to a new consignment of idols: The Osmonds, David Cassidy, The Bay City Rollers. Marc had brought pop music into a new cycle. Now it was turning without him.

Failure in America hurt his self-esteem, and denied him a commercial lifeline. His

friend and rival David Bowie made intelligent use of the space opened up by Marc, and developed his own style in a myriad of intriguing new directions, but Bolan seemed unable or unwilling to change. Pink Floyd and Led Zeppelin were forging vast, ambitious sounds that made Marc's seem timid and cheap. T. Rex fell apart.

Bolan found some personal happiness with his new partner Gloria Jones, but his music rarely impressed and his disillusion deepened. He drank and drugged to excess, which he had never done before, and looked the worse for it. The times changed and Bolan never found a new haircut that suited him. Only in the final days did matters improve: a children's TV series, *Marc*, restored some of his profile, and a national tour, supported by hot new punk band, The Damned, offered him a modicum of credibility.

Even so, the Marc Bolan of those last years cuts a lonely figure, like a little pop Napoleon, plotting his grand return from exile. The punks held him in some affection, sparing him the contempt they felt for most of his contemporaries, but that was largely because he was not a big star any more. He had become merely human Bolan basked in their attention, but he was not one of them. He was really the Last Cavalier in a new age of Roundheads.

Marc died in a car crash, in the early hours of 16 September 1977, just one month after his hero Elvis Presley and two weeks short of his 30th birthday. In a dark, wooded lane in South-west London, you can still see the tree that his car crashed into. It's an eerie memorial, as gothic as anything conceived in Bolan's vividly picturesque imagination and its branches are still permanently decked with tributes left by fans from all over the world.

Musicians, too, honour his memory: R.E.M., Morrissey and Guns'N'Roses are just a few of the acts who've paid homage. Mostly it's the swagger and panache of prime-time Bolan they admire, and it's the music of his peak years that has survived in people's memories. But his recorded legacy is a large one, and there is a wealth of fascination in the details – from the first stirrings of Tyrannosaurus Rex to the last pronouncements of a man out of time. He had more style than substance, but he had plenty of both, and rather more than most. His reign was not a long one, but it was glorious. So long as somebody, somewhere, finds delight in the things he did, then Marc Bolan's spell is still at work.

Paul Du Noyer

INVENTING MARC

• •

The only philosophy I
had as a kid was that a
human being is an art form.
Marc Bolan, 1972

*Even as the young Mark Feld,
growing up in Hackney, Bolan's
sense of presentation and style was
strong, and his self-publicity skills
evident. At the age of fourteen, he
was included in an Evening
Standard article and a Town
magazine feature on mods:*

I've got ten suits, eight sports
jackets, fifteen pairs of slacks, thirty
to thirty-five good shirts, about
twenty jumpers, three leather
jackets, two suede jackets, five or
six pairs of shoes and thirty
exceptionally good ties.
Marc Bolan, 1962

After being expelled from school at fourteen, he drifted through various roles and jobs: a bit of acting, a spate of modelling . . .

I went from being a self-styled cult king to a nobody.
Marc Bolan, 1971

. . . before emerging as a fully-fledged Summer Of Love child in the first version of Tyrannosaurus Rex.

I guess for a while Marc was a good hippie.
Steve Peregrine Took,
Tyrannosaurus Rex, *NME*, 1972

MoDERN iCoNS — MARC BOLAN

His most important re-invention was from cross-legged hippie to glam rock bopper, a blend of elfin bard and strutting peacock that brought him what he knew he'd always desired.

It was fame I wanted – an illusion – like James Dean. I mean, I never thought it would be real. Marc Bolan is an illusion. I'm Mark Feld.
Marc Bolan, *Look-In*, 1974

Marc Bolan. Black, curly hair. Smiles a lot. Hides under bedsheets and imagines technicolor movies. He seemed about four feet high.
Melody Maker, 1968

I'm no longer interested in abstract thought – I'm now living my fantasy . . .
I am what I used to write about on those old albums . . .
I now live that incarnation.
Marc Bolan, *Zigzag*, 1971

He was the inventor of glam – everyone who followed that trail, from Sweet to the New York Dolls, would owe him a debt.

But the glam rock persona was not just show and glitz. Bolan brought his own particular and powerful personal charm to the mix.

On first meeting Marc, I was astounded by the amount of energy he radiated. He lived in a wonderful fantasy world which he never let go of.

Elton John, 1978

It was a physical thing. Like someone had hit me over the head. But that was Marc. He could walk into a room looking like death from the back of beyond, a right little scruff arse! But he still had that charismatic thing.

June Child, later Bolan, on their first encounter

His imagination was sparked off and set off in his mind a great fantasy. Sometimes he had a little difficulty remembering which bits were made up and which weren't.

Simon Napier-Bell, Bolan's first producer

Unlike his friend and rival, David Bowie, who changed like a chameleon to ensure survival, Bolan did not, could not, alter the Marc Bolan he'd created.

Bolan and Bowie had played on each other's recordings – Bolan adding some guitar on Bowie's 'Prettiest Star' in 1970, Bowie helping out on the 'The Slider' and 'Tanx' albums. Their careers were intermingled – and Bowie appeared on Bolan's Granada TV series, Marc, shortly before Bolan died.

Marc brought in the 'Glam' thing, but David took it a step further. Marc sort of stayed at one level of dressing up and wore lamé jackets with musical notations on, and things like that. David came out with these beautiful bizarre costumes from Japan, designed by a top Japanese designer. Marc couldn't think on that level. There was always this envy, this jealousy.

Tony Visconti, producer for Bolan and later Bowie

Marc was well ahead of David Bowie.

T. Rex bassist **Steve Currie**, 1978

FINDING HIS VOICE

● ●

At nine years old I became Elvis Presley.
Marc Bolan

*To complement the outward
display, Bolan blended together
a distinctive musical personality.
Early rock'n'roll was a major
influence, and re-emerged in
the classic T. Rex singles.*

My first experience of rock came when I
heard 'Ballad of Davey Crockett' by Bill
Hayes. My dad went out to buy me a
record and got one by Bill Haley. I was so
disappointed – until I heard the record.
Then I threw Bill Hayes out of the window
and rocked. I've been rockin' ever since.
Marc Bolan, 1970

His rock'n'roll heart was big,
plump and furiously pumping.
NME journalist **Paul Morley,** after Bolan's death.

MoDERN iCoNS – MARC BOLAN

Dylan was the jiver of all time.
Marc Bolan, 1972

*On top of the rock'n'roll, he grafted
the influence of singer-songwriters.
He was a big fan of early Pink
Floyd frontman Syd Barrett, and
admired Donovan, but his main
man was Bob Dylan. One theory
had it that Marc created his stage
surname from BOb dyLAN . . . .*

A lot of people would argue
that Dylan's best stuff was
made around 1963, but to
me his best was 'New
Morning' . . . the first where I
felt that he was actually
giving me his heart – the fact
that the man was prepared to
strip his stomach open and
say 'Look inside, rummage
about, dig me for what I am'.
That's all you can do . . . .
There ain't no more.
Marc Bolan, *Zigzag*, 1971

Dylan has had so much shit laid on him, it's unbelievable. He went electric and got ostracised, he changed style and got ostracised again, he simplified his poetry and imagery and got put down again . . . and all he does is turn his back and say 'get stuffed if you don't like it'. Great!

Marc Bolan, 1971

Bolan's vocal sound was his own distinctive contribution.

Tony Visconti, Bolan's producer, first encountered the man, and his voice, in 1967.

One night I went into the UFO club and saw Tyrannosaurus Rex on stage. There was a very bad PA system but the thing that cut through was Marc's very, very unusual voice, he was very warbly in those days.

Tony Visconti

I think it's horrible. It's like an old pensioner singing.

Trevor Brice of the group Vanity Fare, 1970

If you listen to T. Rex just around the time Mungo Jerry had 'Summertime' as a hit, he'd just made his voice much less wobbly and thinner. All those years, he had it and they took it and made it their gimmick. They made the voice acceptable.

Simon Napier-Bell

ARISE T. REX

After a brief sojourn with hippie outfit John's Children, Bolan started to put his own band together. The first version of Tyrannosaurus Rex featured percussionist Steve Took, who'd answered a Melody Maker ad from Bolan:

Freaky lead guitarist, bass guitarist and drummer wanted for Marc Bolan's new group. Also any other astral flyers like with cars, amplification and that which never grows in window boxes.

With Steve it's very easy because he thinks the way I do. Steve just picks up a drum and bangs away. What the Pink Floyd do electrically, we do acoustically.
Marc Bolan, Melody Maker, 1968

John Peel was an early champion and they were the first unsigned band to appear on Radio 1's Top Gear *in October 1967.*

Marc came round to my flat and sat down on the floor and sang some of his songs. I must say they registered immediately . . . . I knew deep down inside that he was something special.
John Peel, 1978

37

There must be many young men who play bongos and guitars in their pads, sipping wine, smoking endless cigarettes, knocking over piles of Debussy albums, refusing offers of coffee from their chicks . . . Trying to stay awake about 4am, putting ash trays on the tape recorder to make it work – and cursing that they didn't think to make an LP like Marc Bolan and Steve Peregrine Took. The attraction of this simple duo lies in their simplicity, fun and beauty.

Melody Maker review of Tyrannosaurus Rex's debut album, 1968

But after four singles and three albums, Bolan decided that the hippie image – and Took – had to go. The split was announced in October 1969.

We're not playing together any more. There are no bad vibes between us at all. T. Rex is still a very young thing and although it has gone electric, it will still be much softer and more harmonious than most groups.

Marc Bolan, 1969

The credibility of the band was lessened by the fact that people associated us with Flower Power, and that was a long gone era. I wanted people to look at the thing in a new light, and the only way to do that was to have a label change, and change the music, and change the name, but not lose any identity either way.

Marc Bolan,
Creem magazine, 1972

I don't claim to be a guitarist, but I've got flaming hands
and bleeding fingers. I steer the guitar like a ship and sing
with my eyes closed. When I'm bopping it feels great.
Marc Bolan, *Melody Maker*, 1968

What seemed to be the most radical shift,
the move from acoustic to electric guitar, was
not an unexpected change to former colleagues.

He once made a big silver screen out of tinfoil to put
around the amplifiers so it would reflect his feedback,
on gigs. He was totally into Jimi Hendrix at that time
and he loved the electric guitar, so I don't know why he
went back to acoustic guitar when he formed
Tyrannosaurus Rex. I think the reason was basically
because he lost all his equipment when he left the group.
Andy Ellison, lead singer of John's Children

Marc had an alternative theory:
When we started in '67 everyone was doing Cream and
Hendrix, and it was very much hard rock. The only way I could
break through was to be something completely opposite. By the
time it got to be 1970 everyone was playing acoustic . . . .
Marc Bolan

MoDERN iCoNS ● MARC BOLAN

Bolan was not convinced that the duo format needed changing.

In the beginning I was just totally opposed to it, like I am to anything anyone suggests.
Marc Bolan, *Zigzag*, 1971

He did however need a replacement for the sacked Steve Took and found a partner in Mickey Finn, late of Hapshash And The Multi-Coloured Coat.

Marc needed someone who could sing because Steve Took did good harmonies and good backing vocals. Mickey couldn't sing a bloody note, but he looked so splendid and played reasonable bongos . . . . They were very beautiful.
June Bolan

The revitalised T. Rex was enhanced by Mickey Finn's dark brooding looks, and – Bolan having realised he did need to expand the band – bolstered by the rhythm section of Steve Currie and Bill Legend. But not everybody was impressed with Bolan's backing band. The Stones's lead singer caught T. Rex on one US tour:

When I saw 'em in LA I thought the best bit was the acoustic numbers, when he just sat there with his guitar. It was great. But the band . . . Marc Bolan can get away with it, but there's only him. If you don't have a good rhythm section, forget it.

Mick Jagger, 1974

MoDERN iCoNS – MARC BOLAN

The truth of the matter was that Bolan was T. Rex, and his ambition was what drove the whole machine.

Marc was one-directional. He wanted to be famous so he made it happen. Like a blinkered horse he knew exactly where he was going, and how to find the people who would help him get there.

June Bolan

Steve Took was there. Steve Peregrine Took, who used to be in a group called Tyrannosaurus Rex. Remember him? He was walking around not speaking much. Nobody recognised him . . . Marc was running to the safety of his white Rolls Royce.

Michael Watts, *Melody Maker*, 1972 on T. Rex gig in Boston, Lincs

His first manager, Peter Jenner, described him aptly I think. A flower child with a knife up his sleeve.

Tony Visconti

T. REXTASY

All I want to be is myself. I love to dance.
I've always been a bit of a wriggler.
Marc Bolan

*Glam rock arrived, and Bolan was
its first star, some would say its inventor,
before the arrival of anyone else . . .*

Long before Bowie, Glitter or even Alvin Stardust tightened
a single pant, brushed on the first load of non-drip paint,
Our Man Bolan was single-handedly revising the whole
concept of teen idolatry and big boppin' hits.
Chris Welch, *Melody Maker, 1974*

*T. Rex found its audience. And the response was teenybop mania.
The high street sales of glitter, lurex, satin and velvet shot up.*

The way he moves it really gets to me. The curls stick to his
forehead with perspiration. It's so sexy. Everyone is afraid to
step out of line in this world. But not Marc. That's what we
all like about him. He represents what we would like to be.
15-year-old **Noelle Parr**, 1972

*For a heady period, Bolan fans were the
fiercest and most loyal in the industry.*

I can dig him doing this; it's quite nice having
15- and 16-year-old chicks trying to pull
your hair out. But I was just totally freaked out.
Steve Peregrine Took, 1972

I like T. Rex. They seem to be getting to be the new
generation Beatles, with the girls tearing their trousers
off. It's great at first but they'll soon tire of it all.
Paul McCartney, 1971

*The hysteria reached its peak in June 1972, when one fan
suffered a broken jaw, and seats were being demolished.*

It's becoming almost impossible. One more tour, I should
think, and that'll be the last . . . . I haven't been out of my
house for two weeks. It's just like living in a goldfish bowl.
Marc Bolan, *Melody Maker*, 1972

The first time I ever got laid was after a Bolan gig (she
had corkscrew hair, glitter under her eyes, stars on
her cheeks, satin jeans. Phewee! That was a period!).
Paul Morley, *NME*, 1977

MoDERN iCoNS ● MARC BOLAN

But the ecstasy gave way to agony as Bolan's formula ran out of steam, and the US teeny idols The Osmonds and David Cassidy took over.

Dick Clark the American Bandstand presenter, told critic Lester Bangs that Bolan had been guilty of self-delusion.

He thought he was Mick Jagger. He was Donny Osmond . . . . The trouble was, the poor fellow believed his own publicity, when you had Ringo Starr running around taking pictures of him with an 8-millimeter camera.

He's been so many things in his career I don't guess he knows who he is. And he has been so ill-advised – this happens with so many artistic people – a man of obviously great talents, but no business acumen. And so therefore never the twain shall cross, and he went into the sewer.

Dick Clark, *Creem* magazine, 1973

51

THE POETRY MAN

*Bolan frequently cited the
importance of literature in his self-
education, from Wordsworth to
Dylan Thomas, Rimbaud to Keats.*

Just to glance through his
bookshelves is enough
indication of the areas of
thought he has studied. Poetry,
science fiction, mysticism, horror,
magic and Eastern thought are
all well represented and one
small pile of books contains the
life stories or rock 'greats' such
as Elvis, Adam Faith, Tommy
Steele and The Beatles.
Beat Instrumental magazine

He didn't read much at all.
Books had to be read to him
Tony Visconti, 1978

*Sometimes it was best just
to let Bolan explain.*

Sharks-fin-soup-in-Paraguay.
Terrapin.
Inconspicuous-limp.
Food-blender.
Chaise-longue.
Marc Bolan, asked by Paul Morley
what his five favourite words were

I want to do a Marc Bolan album,
but I don't know what it is yet. Might
be a spoken word album, it might
just be me cracking eggs with loads
of echo . . .
Marc Bolan, *NME*, March 1977

I get a stream of inspiration and my
hand writes away, and the words
don't always make sense. They fit
like an abstract painting.
Marc Bolan, *Melody Maker*, 1968

Science fiction and fantasy was another favourite source. His first Tyrannosaurus Rex partner Steve Peregrine Took had taken his name from Tolkien's Lord Of The Rings.

I believe elves existed. Not as elves, but as strong, wise, people, like the Atlanteans. I believe in the magic of life . . . The elf people have died out or walked off the earth into a rainbow. Only the people who wear metal underwear or have black blood are left.

Marc Bolan to journalist Chris Welch, *Melody Maker*

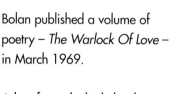

Bolan published a volume of poetry – *The Warlock Of Love* – in March 1969.

A lot of people think that because I've got away from long visual descriptions that I'm no longer a poet, but what I'm writing now is poetry of the heart really, and I'm much more interested in that now . . . Two years ago I was very into being a poet and I'm not any more because I am a poet . . . I've now become Marc Bolan, in fact, which I never was before.

Marc Bolan, *Zigzag*, 1971

Listen, the man was poet.

Cockney Rebel's **Steve Harley**

Everything I do is poetry to music.

Marc Bolan

THE COSMIC PUNK

None of the albums were written under drugs. I took acid about four times in 1970 but I didn't like it. I was spiked with STP and was under sedation for two weeks. I came out and wrote 'Ride A White Swan'.

Marc Bolan

Although Bolan later sank into heavy drinking and bingeing, as his glam rock crown slipped, he claimed that his early writing was simply inspired by imagination and being high on being Marc. In fact, Took's drug-taking was one of the major reasons he was dropped from T. Rex – it interfered with Bolan's drive for success.

Steve Took was very heavy into acid, but very heavy; not just an indulger but he was taking two or three trips a day. He became just like a vegetable and on stage he would suddenly start taking his clothes off and beating himself with belts. We left Steve in America; we abandoned him.

June Bolan, 1978

*If drug-taking was not part of the original Marc Bolan character,
then teasing people with his sexuality was.*

I'm bisexual but I believe I'm heterosexual, 'cos I definitely like
boobs. I always wish I were a hundred per cent gay; it's much
easier, but not much fun. Anyway I checked it out and I prefer chicks.
Record Mirror 1975

The undoubted instigator of the glam rock craze – androgyny, pop
and style was the late Marc Bolan . . . . The biggest teen idol since
the Walker Brothers and the first major star since Hendrix to
emphasise sexuality and visual image.
NME 1977

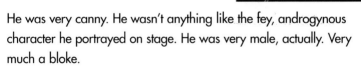

All this thing about him being gay in the
papers came later, because it was
fashionable to say you were. But he
actually loathed making love to men.
June Bolan

He was very canny. He wasn't anything like the fey, androgynous
character he portrayed on stage. He was very male, actually. Very
much a bloke.
Photographer **Kieron 'Spud' Murphy**, *Q* magazine, 1995

MoDERN iCoNS – MARC BOLAN

*The glitter round the eyes, the
flamboyance, was all part of the image
and set the agenda for all the subsequent
androgynous clones.*

Overt sexuality is not a strong facet of
Bolan's appeal. Sex is part of it, but it's
sex courtesy of The Magic Prince, who's
going to deflower the young virgin in an
atmosphere of blissful romance.

Phil McNeill, *NME*, 1972

I bet you thought,
'He's a right little poof', didn't you?

Bolan to policeman who'd
commented on his eye make-up

He was a sculpted,
not line-drawn,
animated rock star;
fluffy cloud pretty,
groovy-fun-cosmic,
indulgent, arrogant,
stylish, the ultimate
poser, boaster,
leader-onner, leader.
Paul Morley, *NME*, 1977

Inside the 'freak' was a family man. His wife June centred and stabilised him, before they split in 1973. And with subsequent girlfriend, singer Gloria Jones, he became a father in 1975. His son was named Rolan Bolan: shades of Zowie Bowie. The family unit consisted of three Librans, which he liked to point out.

She was very much part of the whole thing, and a lot of the ideas came from her. She was a very creative force, as Yoko was with John.

Photographer **Kieron Murphy**,
1995, on June Bolan's influence

I delivered him myself. Very expertly, too. This baby's made all the difference to my life. I was nearly over the edge. I'd had five nervous breakdowns and gone crazy about eight times.

Marc Bolan, on his son's birth

He had always used the word punk to describe himself, a pick-up from American. The Damned supported him on tour in early 1977.

Listen, I was the originator of Punk Rock. We had a big sign on the Strip that read, 'The Cosmic Punk Comes', and no one got it.
Marc Bolan, *Record Mirror*, 1976

He was one of our biggest inspirations, one of our few pop idols. When he was at his peak, all today's punks were just waking up to music and he was one of the biggest influences on them.
Rat Scabies, The Damned

The Damned I like a lot. I was introduced to them because one of them had the good taste to wear a Marc Bolan T-shirt.
Marc Bolan, 1977

I was more sad when I heard about Marc Bolan than Elvis.
Tony James, Generation X

69

MUSICAL MOMENTS

· ·

*Bolan's first real chart success was 'Ride A White Swan',
which reached Number Two in late 1970.*

'Ride A White Swan' was the turning point. It was really a
science-fiction story I wrote – now I keep all of that sort of
material for my poetry books and concentrate on street songs.

Marc Bolan

This must be a hit or I'll eat my toadstool.
On second thoughts – mushroom.

Chris Welch, *Melody Maker, 1970*

He made some classic pop singles: I remember jamming a
crummy transistor to my ear to catch the fey electric mystique of
the unashamedly simplistic 'Ride A White Swan', rushing out to
buy it, and not even having a record player.

Paul Morley, 1977

Doubtless you'll own it before long – if you don't by Christmas,
my flock of highly trained hedgehogs will fan out through the
land and retribution will be swift and terrible – indeed it will . . . .

John Peel

1971 was Bolan's annus mirabilis: his first Number Ones, with 'Hot Love' and 'Get It On', and 'Jeepster' only just missing the top spot. In that year, T. Rex represented 3.5% of all British record sales.

I've suddenly tuned into that mental channel which makes a record a hit and I feel at present as though I could write Number Ones for ever. Let's face it, the majority of pop hits that make it are a permutation on the twelve-bar blues and I've found one that works.

Marc Bolan, 1971

He was an amazing rhythm guitarist. If you listen to 'Hot Love' and 'Get It On', they're classics of really four to the bar, straight foot-tappers.

Steve Currie

'Hot love' I wrote because I wanted to write a rock record. I know it's exactly like a million other songs, but I hope it's got a little touch of me in it too.

Marc Bolan, *Zigzag*, 1971

Bolan's boogie. It's an understated shuffle beat, monotonous, but compulsive. Marc sings mysteriously, and is backed by stomping drums and trundling guitars.

Norman Smith, *Melody Maker*, 1971

MoDERN iCoNS ⬤ MARC BOLAN

1971's 'Electric Warrior' was the album that marked T. Rex's transition from the folky hippie feel of the early recordings to full-on rock'n'roll.

As far as I'm concerned, it's the first album I've ever made; the others were just ideas, but in this one I spoke about me, and you, and all of us.

Marc Bolan

A strong black album cover depicting Marc Bolan in a golden Ready Brek aura. It wasn't just the dark cellos or the breathy vocals, but something intangibly sexual. This album made me tease my hair and get my first guitar.

Holly Johnson, *Q* magazine, 1995

It's probably the loosest album I've ever recorded because it was done between gigs in America and I was essentially concerned with putting down rough tracks to establish a sound, but they felt so good that we kept them for the finished track.

Marc Bolan

Quaint and curious twisting of the skeins of pop, a gathering and weaving, which makes it not in the least significant, but decidedly enjoyable.

Melody Maker, 1971

75

MoDERN iCoNS ● MARC BOLAN

After the high point of 1971-72, Bolan never quite recaptured the success of the T. Rextasy days.

'The Slider' was an understatement, a limited cultural scan but still a marvellous mix'n'match bubble rock album.
Paul Morley, *NME*, 1977

I won't stand and be jeered at when I'm doing something that's a craft I've worked hard on for seven years or more. I've never felt so insecure or such pain as I do now, because I'm so exposed musically.
Bolan, on the release of 'Tanx', 1973

When I run into serious trouble I'll sit down and knock you out five hits – well easy, no problem.

Marc Bolan, *NME*, 1974

IN MEMORIAM

Bolan's death is one of rock and pop's litany of early departures. Like Richie Valens and Buddy Holly's plane crash, or Eddie Cochran's auto accident, it preserved him as an immortal youth, and the elements – the purple Mini GT, the tree on Barnes Common – became 20th century saintly relics.

The accident occurred at 05:58, September 16th 1977.

Richmond Accident Administration Unit

Bolan died when the Mini in which he was passenger, with Gloria at the wheel, crashed into a tree in Barnes, South-west London, last Friday morning. The crash occurred at a notorious accident black spot on the far side of a hump-back bridge and on a wet surface. Bolan himself did not drive and had never held a licence.

NME, 24 September 1977

IN MEMORIAM

I honestly feel it could all end tomorrow. Not just the band thing. I mean life. I could have my hands blown off, and that'd be it.
Marc Bolan, 1970

As Marc would have said, rocking back on his heels, teeth flashing – 'What a way to go. Heaven's hot at the moment'.
Paul Morley, *NME*, 1977

I don't think Marc is unhappy. The only thing that is happening up there is that Marc is telling Elvis how to sing and Jimi how to play
Gloria Jones

MoDERN iCoNS – MARC BOLAN

Marc was a star. He was always
a star. And he wanted to live.
Tony Howard, Bolan's manager

He's a hard cat to describe. He's
very special and he knows it. If he
met God they'd fight it out
together. 'When I meet God I
might cry but I wouldn't be
humble' he's said.
B. P. Fallon, publicist for T. Rex, 1972

Keep a little Marc in your heart.
Badge worn by grieving fans

MoDERN iCoNS ● MARC BOLAN

I do believe in reincarnation; I've
been back about three times that I
know of.
Marc Bolan, 1975

Two weeks after Marc's death I
suddenly conceived. I've no idea
why. Marc always had this thing
about reincarnation.
June Bolan, *NME*, 1978

THE MUSIC

★★★★★   Essential listening
★★★   OK
★   Frankly, not the best!

SINGLES

Solo:
The Wizard/Beyond The Rising Sun – November 1965 ★★★
Hippy Gumbo/Misfit – December 1966 ★★1/2

John's Children:
Desdemona/Remember Thomas A Beckett – May 1967 ★★★★

Tyrannosaurus Rex:
Debora/Child Star – April 1968 ★★★★

T. Rex:
Ride A White Swan/Is It Love/Summertime Blues – October 1970 ★★★★1/2
Hot Love/King Of The Mountain Cometh/Woodland Rock – February 1971 ★★★★★
Get It On/There Was A Time/Raw Ramp – July 1971 ★★★★★
Jeepster/Life's A Gas – November 1971 ★★★1/2
Telegram Sam/Baby Strange/Cadillac – January 1972 ★★★★★
Metal Guru/Lady/Thunderwing – May 1972 ★★★★
Children Of The Revolution/Jitterbug Love/Sunken Rags – September 1972 ★★1/2
Sold Gold Easy Action/Born To Boogie – December 1972 ★★
Twentieth Century Boy/Free Angel – March 1973 ★★★★
Teenage Dream/Satisfaction Pony – January 1974 ★★★★
Zip Gun Boogie/Space Boss – February 1975 ★★
I Love To Boogie/Baby Boomerang – June 1976 ★★★

ALBUMS

Tyrannosaurus Rex:
My People Were Fair And Had Sky In Their Hair . . . But Now They're Content To Wear Stars On Their Brows – June 1968 ★★★1/2
Hot Rod Momma/Scenescof/Child Star/Strange Orchestras/Chateau in Virginia Waters/Dwarfish Trumpet Blues/Mustang Ford/Afghan Woman/Knight/Graceful Fat Sheba/Weilder Of Words/Frowning Atahuallpa (My Inca Love)

Prophets Seers And Sages, The Angels Of The Ages
 – October 1968 ★★★
Deboraarobed/Stacy Grove/Wind Quartets/Consuela/Trelawny Lawn/ Aznageel the Mage/The Friends/Salamanda Palaganda/Our Wonderful Brown–Skin Man/Oh Harley (The Saltimbanques)/Eastern Spell/ The Travelling Tragition/Juniper Suction/Scenes Of Dynasty

Unicorn – May 1969 ★★★1/2
Chariots Of Silk/'Pon A Hill/The Seal Of Seasons/The Throat Of Winter/ Cat Black (The Wizards Hat)/Stones For Avalon/She Was Born To Be My Unicorn/Like A White Star Tangled And Far/Tulip That's What You Are/ Warlord Of The Royal Crocodiles/Evenings of Damask/Iscariot/Nijinsky Hind/The Pilgrim's Tale/The Misty Coast Of Albany/Romany Soup

A Beard Of Stars – March 1970 ★★★★
Prelude/A Day Laye/The Woodland Bop/Fist Heart Mighty Dawn Dart/Pavilions Of Sun/Organ Blues/By The Light Of The Magical Moon/Wind Cheetah/A Beard Of Stars/Great Horse/Dragon's Ear/Lofty Skies/Dove/Elemental Child

T. Rex:
T. Rex – December 1970 ★★★★
The Children Of Rarn/Jewel/The Visit/Childe/The Time Of Love Is Now/Diamond Meadows/Root Of Star/Beltane Walk/Is It Love?/One Inch Rock/Summer Deep/Seagull Woman/Suneye/The Wizard/Children Of Rarn (reprise)

MoDERN iCoNS - MARC BOLAN

Electric Warrior – September 1971 ★★★★★
Mambo Sun/Cosmic Dancer/Jeepster/Monolith/Lean Woman Blues/Get It
On/Planet Queen/Girl/The Motivator/Life's A Gas/Rip Off

The Slider – July 1972 ★★★★★
Metal Guru/Mystic Lady/Rock On/The Slider/Baby Boomerang/Spaceball
Ricochet/Buick Mackane/Telegram Sam/Rabbit Fighter/Baby Strange/Ballrooms
Of Mars/Chariot Choogle/Main Man

Tanx – March 1973 ★★★
Tenement Lady/Rapids/Mister Mister/Broken Hearted Blues/Country
Honey/Electric Slim And The Factory Hen/Mad Donna/Born To Boogie/Life Is
Strange/The Street And Babe Shadow/Highway Knees/Left Hand Luke

Zinc Alloy And The Hidden Riders Of Tomorrow – March 1974 ★★1/2
Venus Loon/Sound Pit/Explosive Mouth/Nameless Wilderness/Painless Persuasion
V/The Meathawk Immaculate/The Avengers (Superbad)/The Leopards Featuring
Gardenia And The Mighty Slug/Galaxy/Change/Liquid Gang/Carsmile Smith
And The Old One/You Got To Jive To Stay Alive/Spanish Midnight/Interstellar
Soul/Teenage Dream

Bolan Zip Gun – February 1975 ★★1/2
Light Of Love/Solid Baby/Precious Star/Token Of My Love/Space Boss/Think
Zink/Till Dawn/Girl In The Thunderbolt Suit/I Really Love You Babe/Golden
Belt/Zip Gun Boogie

Futuristic Dragon – February 1976 ★★
Intro-Futuristic Dragon/Jupiter Liar/Chrome Sitar/All Alone/New York City/My
Little Baby/Calling All Destroyers/Theme For A Dragon/Sensation Boulevard/Ride
My Wheels/Dreamy Lady/Dawn Storm/Casual Agent

Dandy In The Underworld – March 1977 ★★1/2
Dandy In The Underworld/Crimson Moon/Universe/I'm A Fool For You Girl/I
Love To Boogie/Visions Of Domino/Jason B. Sad/Groove A Little/Soul Of My
Suit/Hang-Ups/Pain And Love/Teen Riot Structure

THE HISTORY

Key Dates

30 September 1947
Born in Hackney Hospital, East London, the second
son of Phyllis and Syd Feld. Christened Mark.

September 1962
Appears in *Town* magazine feature on mods.

Age 14
Expelled from school – after school: various jobs including small acting parts,
modelling, serving in a clothes shop, an unsuccessful attempt to break into the
music business as Toby Tyler.

September 1965
First single with Decca, 'The Wizard/Beyond The Rising Sun' under the name
Marc Bowland. Appears on Ready, Steady Go!

November 1966
Links up with producer Simon Napier-Bell, and records 'Hippy Gumbo' for EMI.

March 1967
Joins John's Children, a Napier-Bell act, for a couple of months, during which time
he writes their single 'Desdemona', and appears with them at the 14-Hour
Technicolor Dream at Alexandra Palace.

July 1967
Debut of Tyrannosaurus Rex with new partner Steve Took.

February 1968
Deal signed with Tony Visconti, producer, with first single 'Debora' released May.

July 1968
First Tyrannosaurus Rex album 'My People
Were Fair...' released – reaches 15 in UK charts.

MoDERN iCoNS - MARC BOLAN

March 1969
Bolan's poetry collection – *The Warlock Of Love* – published.

October 1969
Took replaced by Mickey Finn.

1970
Marries June Child.

Oct 1970
'Ride A White Swan' released, goes to Number 2
in the UK. Tyrannosaurus Rex reborn as T. Rex.

Dec 1970
Steve Currie joins on bass, to be joined by Bill Legend on drums.

March 1971
'Hot Love' released. Becomes T. Rex's first Number 1 (for six weeks).

July 1971
'Get It On' also reaches Number 1 – and is the biggest international hit for the
group, released 1972 in the US as 'Bang A Gong', since the group Chase had put
out a single called 'Get In On' in 1971.

October 1971
'Electric Warrior' album released, the first as the new T. Rex, goes to Number 1 in
the UK.

July 1972
'The Slider' released, the most successful T. Rex album in the States.

T. Rextasy at its height.

December 1972
Premiere of 'Born To Boogie', Ringo Star's Apple documentary on T. Rex, featuring
footage shot at 2 sell-out concerts at Empire Pool Wembley in March 1972.

July 1973
Along with additional musicians, Gloria Jones joins T. Rex as a backing vocalist.

January 1974
First major UK tour for two years – the 'Truck Off' tour.

March 1974
Bolan parts company with producer Tony Visconti.

Feb 1975
Mickey Finn quits T. Rex.

September 1975
Rolan Seymour Feld Bolan born to Bolan and Gloria Jones.

July 1976
'I Love To Boogie' released, Bolan's last UK Top 20 hit.

Autumn 1976
Tour of the UK supported by The Damned.

March 1977
The last T. Rex live gig, at the Locarno, Portsmouth.

April 1977
'Dandy In The Underworld', the final album, released.

16 September 1977
Bolan is killed instantly as a passenger in a Mini driven by Gloria Jones. The car hits a tree on Barnes Common in the early hours of the morning.

THE BOOKS

Marc Bolan: Born To Boogie – Chris Welch & Simon Napier-Bell (Eel Pie) 1982

Marc Bolan: The Legendary Years – John & Shan Bramley (Smith Gryphon) 1992

Marc Bolan: Wilderness Of The Mind – John Williams & Caron Thomas
        (Xanadu) 1992

Electric Warrior: The Marc Bolan Story – Paul Sinclair (Omnibus) 1982

Twentieth Century Boy: The Marc Bolan Story – Mark Paytress
        (Sidgwick & Jackson) 1992

THE CAST

June Bolan, née Child. Marc's first wife. They meet when he approaches Pink Floyd's managers, Blackhill Enterprises, in 1967, asking them to represent him. June is Blackhill's general factotum. Marc and June marry in 1970, but separate in 1973.

Steve Currie. Born 20 May 1947, Grimsby. Joins T. Rex as bassist (having played with various groups including home town band The Rumble) in December 1970 as Bolan expands the group. After leaving T. Rex in 1976, he moves to Portugal, where he dies in a car crash in April 1981.

Mickey Finn. Born 3 June 1947, Thornton Heath, Surrey. Had been conga player with Hapshash And The Coloured Coat before responding to Bolan's ad seeking a replacement for Steve Took. Stays with T. Rex until 1975. Subsequently plays occasional sessions, including with the Blow Monkeys.

John's Children. The band Bolan joins in 1967, at the time an underground flower-power group born in 1966 out of a mod band called The Silence. After Bolan leaves, they put out a couple more singles, but then split. Vocalist Andy Ellison re-appears with the pop/punk Radio Stars in 1977. Drummer John Hewlett later manages Sparks.

Gloria Jones. Born 19 September 1947, Ohio. Singer in the musical 'Hair' where she first meets Bolan on tour. They meet again when she becomes a backing singer for T. Rex in 1973. They get together, and have a child, Rolan, in 1975. She is at the wheel of the Mini that crashes in September 1977. She survives, Bolan is killed.

Bill Legend. Born Bill Fyfield, 8 May 1944, Barking. Joins T. Rex shortly after Steve Currie comes in as bassist – he is recruited from a Southend band called Legend, hence Bolan's nickname for him. Leaves T. Rex in 1973 (replaced by Davy Lutton) and returns to the pub rock circuit.

Simon Napier-Bell. Producer of the Yardbirds and John's Children who signs up Bolan, adds him to the John's Children line-up, and produces the early Tyrannosaurus Rex singles. After retiring in the early Seventies, returns to manage Wham! and Japan.

Steve Peregrine Took. Born Stephen Potter, 28 July 1949 in Eltham, Kent. Joins Tyrannosaurus Rex in its first manifestation and provides bongo backing to Bolan. Fired in 1969, he does little thereafter, putting half-hearted bands together in Ladbroke Grove. Dies in October 1980, a drug-related asphyxiation. A friend's verdict: "He just never made a serious attempt to get himself together."

T. Rex. Other musicians who featured in the later life of Bolan's band include drummer Davy Lutton who goes on to work with Wreckless Eric; guitarist Jack Green who subsequently plays with The Pretty Things; and bassist Herbie Flowers, one of the great session bass players, who is part of John Williams's Sky.

Tony Visconti. Born 24 April 1944, Brooklyn, NY. Sees Tyrannosaurus Rex at UFO in 1967, produces their first album in four days flat. Works with Bolan and T. Rex until 1974. Makes his name with them, and subsequently by producing David Bowie (he plays bass on 'The Man Who Sold The World'). Works widely with vast range of acts from Gentle Giant to Iggy Pop and the Stranglers to Mary Hopkin (whom he married).

PICTURE CREDITS